GW00459323

CONGRATULATIONS YOU'RE 50

summersdale

CONGRATULATIONS YOU'RE 50

First published 2014 as *50 and Proud of It*

With text contributed by Vicky Edwards

Summersdale Publishers Ltd
46 West Street
Chichester
West Sussex
PO19 1RP
UK

www.summersdale.com

Printed and bound in the Czech Republic

ISBN: 978-1-84953-903-6

Substantial discounts on bulk quantities of Summersdale books are available to corporations, professional associations and other organisations. For details contact Nicky Douglas by telephone: +44 (0) 1243 756902, fax: +44 (0) 1243 786300 or email: nicky@summersdale.com.

To...

From...

CONTENTS

ANOTHER YEAR OLDER

By the time we
hit 50... we have
learned to take
life seriously, but
never ourselves.

Marie Dressler

We're vintage!

Jennifer Saunders and Dawn French
on both reaching 50

Happy twentieth anniversary of your thirtieth birthday!

Anonymous

It takes a long time to become young.

Pablo Picasso

As a graduate of
the Zsa Zsa Gabor
School of Creative
Mathematics, I
honestly do not
know how old I am.

Erma Bombeck

Forty is the old age of youth; 50 the youth of old age.

Victor Hugo

To me, old age is always 15 years older than I am.

Bernard M. Baruch

About the only thing that comes to us without effort is old age.

Gloria Pitzer

I'd like to grow very old as slowly as possible.

Charles Lamb

How old would you be if you didn't know how old you are?

Satchel Paige

The woman who
tells her age is
either too young
to have anything
to lose or too old
to have anything
to gain.

Chinese proverb

I refuse to admit
I'm more than 52,
even if that does
make my sons
illegitimate.

Nancy Astor

**Few women
admit their
age. Few men
act theirs.**

Anonymous

No woman
should ever be
quite accurate about
her age. It looks
so calculating.

Oscar Wilde

For all the advances in medicine, there is still no cure for the common birthday.

John Glenn

For years I wanted to be older, and now I am.

Margaret Atwood

You know you're
getting old when
the candles cost
more than the cake.

Bob Hope

Just remember,
once you're over the
hill you begin to
pick up speed.

Arthur Schopenhauer

JUST WHAT
I ALWAYS
WANTED

Youth is the gift of nature, but age is a work of art.

Garson Kanin

A comfortable old
age is the reward
of a well-spent
youth.

Maurice Chevalier

Yesterday is history, tomorrow is a mystery, but today is a gift. That is why it is called the present.

Alice Morse Earle

A gift,
with a kind
countenance,
is a double
present.

Thomas Fuller

**Every wrinkle is
but a notch in the
quiet calendar of a
well-spent life.**

Charles Dickens

**Each day comes
bearing its own
gifts. Untie the
ribbons.**

Ruth Ann Schabacker

A true friend remembers your birthday but not your age.

Anonymous

Age is just a
number. It's totally
irrelevant unless,
of course, you
happen to be a
bottle of wine.

Joan Collins

A friend never
defends a husband
who gets his wife
an electric skillet
for her birthday.

Erma Bombeck

The ability to laugh, especially at ourselves, keeps the heart light and the mind young.

Anonymous

No one is so old as
to think he cannot
live one more year.

Cicero

No wise man ever wished to be younger.

Jonathan Swift

There are 364 days
when you might
get un-birthday
presents... and only
one for birthday
presents, you know.

Lewis Carroll

You know you're
getting old when
the only thing
you want for your
birthday is not to
be reminded of it.

Anonymous

GRIN AND BEAR IT

If I'd known
I was going to live
this long, I'd have
taken better care
of myself.

Eubie Blake

If you find yourself
50 years old and
you aren't doing
what you love, then
what's the point?

Jim Carrey

Whenever the talk turns to age, I say I am 49 plus VAT.

Lionel Blair

The years teach much which the days never knew.

Ralph Waldo Emerson

Another belief of mine: that everyone else my age is an adult, whereas I am merely in disguise.

Margaret Atwood

Perhaps one has to be very old before one learns to be amused rather than shocked.

Pearl S. Buck

Nice to be here?
At my age it's nice
to be anywhere.

George Burns

Ageing is not 'lost youth' but a new stage of opportunity and strength.

Betty Friedan

It is a mistake
to regard age as
a downhill grade
toward dissolution.
The reverse is true.
As one grows older,
one climbs with
surprising strides.

George Sand

I'm like old wine.
They don't bring me
out very often, but
I'm well preserved.

Rose Kennedy

I believe in loyalty.
I think when a
woman reaches an
age she likes, she
should stick to it.

Eva Gabor

Age is something that doesn't matter, unless you are a cheese.

Luis Buñuel

My mother is going
to have to stop
lying about her age
because pretty soon
I'm going to be
older than she is.

Tripp Evans

Zeal, *n.* A certain nervous disorder afflicting the young and inexperienced.

Ambrose Bierce

DO A LITTLE DANCE, MAKE A LITTLE LOVE

**Old people aren't
exempt from having
fun and dancing...
and playing.**

Liz Smith

There's a kind of
confidence that
comes when you're
in your forties and
fifties, and men
find that incredibly
attractive.

Peggy Northrop

Middle age is having a choice between two temptations and choosing the one that'll get you home earlier.

Dan Bennett

It's sex, not youth, that's wasted on the young.

Janet Harris

One of the signs
of passing youth is
the birth of a sense
of fellowship with
other human beings
as we take our place
among them.

Virginia Woolf

You know you're
knocking on when
you feel like the
morning-after-
the-night-before
without having
been anywhere.

Anonymous

The young sow wild oats. The old grow sage.

Winston Churchill

I'll keep swivelling
my hips until they
need replacing.

Tom Jones

I'm limitless as far
as age is concerned
– as long as he has
a driver's licence.

*Kim Cattrall on dating
younger men*

Old wood best to
burn, old wine to
drink, old friends
to trust, and old
authors to read.

Francis Bacon

A man is a fool if he drinks before he reaches 50, and a fool if he doesn't drink afterward.

Frank Lloyd Wright

We've both hit 50,
and we celebrate it.
There is no doomy
side to it... We're
nearly grown-up
now, but not quite.

*Dawn French and
Jennifer Saunders*

May you live all the days of your life.

Jonathan Swift

If you think hitting 40 is liberating, wait till you hit 50.

Michelle Pfeiffer

YOUNG AT
HEART

You can't turn
back the clock.
But you can wind
it up again.

Bonnie Prudden

The great thing about getting older is that you don't lose all the other ages you've been.

Madeleine L'Engle

The old believe everything; the middle-aged suspect everything: the young know everything.

Oscar Wilde

Children are a
great comfort in
your old age - and
they help you reach
it faster, too.

Lionel Kauffman

A young man is embarrassed to question an older one.

Homer

Growing old is
no more than a
bad habit which a
busy man has no
time to form.

André Maurois

I'm surprised that
I'm 50... I still feel
like a kid.

Bruce Willis

When grace is joined
with wrinkles, it is
adorable. There is an
unspeakable dawn in
happy old age.

Victor Hugo

With age comes the inner, the higher life. Who would be forever young, to dwell always in externals?

Elizabeth Cady Stanton

As is a tale,
so is life: not
how long it is, but
how good it is, is
what matters.

Seneca

A man is not old as long as he is seeking something.

Jean Rostand

One of the
best parts of
growing older?
You can flirt all
you like since
you've become
harmless.

Liz Smith

OLDER AND WISER?

If you carry
your childhood
with you, you never
become older.

Tom Stoppard

To know how
to grow old is
the masterwork
of wisdom.

Henri-Frédéric Amiel

Young men's
minds are always
changeable, but
when an old man
is concerned in a
matter, he looks
both before
and after.

Homer

The best way to
get most husbands
to do something
is to suggest that
perhaps they're too
old to do it.

Ann Bancroft

The ageing process
has you firmly
in its grasp if
you never get the
urge to throw a
snowball.

Doug Larson

Old age puts
more wrinkles in
our minds than
on our faces.

Michel de Montaigne

Love has more depth as you get older.

Kirk Douglas

You are only young
once, but you can be
immature for
a lifetime.

John P. Grier

He's so old that
when he orders a
three-minute egg,
they ask for the
money up front.

Milton Berle

I have enjoyed greatly the second blooming... suddenly you find - at the age of 50, say - that a whole new life has opened before you.

Agatha Christie

Becoming a
grandmother is
wonderful. One
moment you're just
a mother. The next
you are all-wise
and prehistoric.

Pam Brown

The surprising thing about young fools is how many survive to become old fools.

Doug Larson

No man is ever old enough to know better.

Holbrook Jackson

Before you contradict an old man, my fair friend, you should endeavour to understand him.

George Santayana

Age is whatever you think it is. You are as old as you think you are.

Muhammad Ali

I'm aiming by
the time I'm 50
to stop being
an adolescent.

Wendy Cope

LIVE, LOVE
AND LAST

**No man
loves life like
him that's
growing old.**

Sophocles

**Nobody grows
old merely by
living a number
of years. We grow
old by deserting
our ideals.**

Samuel Ullman

I don't believe in ageing. I believe in forever altering one's aspect to the sun.

Virginia Woolf

The follies which
a man regrets most
in his life are those
which he didn't
commit when he had
the opportunity.

Helen Rowland

The other day
a man asked me
what I thought
was the best time
of life. 'Why,' I
answered... 'now.'

David Grayson

Middle age is when we can do just as much as ever – but would rather not.

Anonymous

Tomorrow's gone – we'll have tonight!

Dorothy Parker

Years may wrinkle
the skin, but to
give up enthusiasm
wrinkles the soul.

Samuel Ullman

The time to begin most things is ten years ago.

Mignon McLaughlin

I look forward to growing old and wise and audacious.

Glenda Jackson

He who laughs, lasts!

Mary Pettibone Poole

The purpose of life is to fight maturity.

Dick Werthimer

**Age does not
protect you from
love. But love,
to some extent,
protects you
from age.**

Jeanne Moreau

The average child
laughs about 400
times per day,
the average adult
laughs only 15
times per day.

Anonymous

ILLS, PILLS AND TWINGES

Time doth flit;
oh shit!

Dorothy Parker

I don't feel old. I
don't feel anything
till noon. That's
when it's time
for my nap.

Bob Hope

My doctor told me to do something that puts me out of breath, so I've taken up smoking again.

Jo Brand

You know you've
reached middle-
age when your
weightlifting
consists merely of
standing up.

Bob Hope

Middle age is when
you choose your
cereal for the fibre,
not the toy.

Anonymous

The years between
50 and 70 are the
hardest. You are
always being asked
to do more, and yet
you are not decrepit
enough to turn
them down.

T. S. Eliot

I would rather be round and jolly than thin and cross.

Ann Widdecombe

I feel stronger
now than, maybe,
20 years ago...
If your mind is
strong, your body
will be strong.

Madonna

Middle age is the time when a man is always thinking that in a week or two he will feel as good as ever.

Don Marquis

To win back my
youth, there is
nothing I wouldn't
do – except take
exercise, get up
early, or be a useful
member of the
community.

Oscar Wilde

Old minds are like old horses; you must exercise them if you wish to keep them in working order.

John Quincy Adams

I never worry
about diets. The
only carrots that
interest me are the
number you get in
a diamond.

Mae West

Old age ain't no
place for sissies.

Bette Davis

As you get older three things happen. The first is your memory goes, and I can't remember the other two...

Norman Wisdom

Age seldom arrives smoothly or quickly. It's more often a succession of jerks.

Jean Rhys

**What most persons
consider as virtue,
after the age of
40 is simply a loss
of energy.**

Voltaire

CHIN UP,
CHEST OUT

You can only
perceive real beauty
in a person as they
get older.

Anouk Aimée

The secret of
staying young is
to live honestly,
eat slowly and lie
about your age.

Lucille Ball

The age of a woman
doesn't mean a
thing. The best
tunes are played on
the oldest fiddles.

Ralph Waldo Emerson

Good cheekbones are the brassiere of old age.

Barbara de Portago

I don't plan to grow
old gracefully.
I plan to have
facelifts until my
ears meet.

Rita Rudner

You know you're
getting old when
you stoop to tie
your shoes and
wonder what else
you can do while
you're down there.

George Burns

Anyone who keeps the ability to see beauty never grows old.

Franz Kafka

Please don't retouch my wrinkles. It took me so long to earn them.

Anna Magnani

When it comes to
staying young, a
mind-lift beats a
facelift any day.

Marty Bucella

The longer I live the more beautiful life becomes.

Frank Lloyd Wright

One of the
many things
nobody ever tells
you about middle
age is that it's such
a nice change from
being young.

Dorothy Canfield Fisher

I'm not
denying my age,
I'm embellishing
my youth.

Tamara Reynolds

Let us respect grey hairs, especially our own.

J. P. Sears

Nature gives you
the face you have
at 20, but it's up to
you to merit the
face you have at 50.

Coco Chanel

She was a
handsome woman
of 45 and would
remain so for
many years.

Anita Brookner

**Middle age is when
your age starts
to show around
your middle.**

Bob Hope

It is not how old you are, but how you are old.

Marie Dressler

There is no old age.
There is, as there
always was,
just you.

Carol Matthau

If you're interested in
finding out more about our
books, find us on Facebook at
Summersdale Publishers and
follow us on Twitter at
@Summersdale.

www.summersdale.com